Python For Data Analysis

A Complete Beginner Guide to Wrangling & Analyzing Data Using Python

Craig Berg

Introduction

Python is one of the best and most utilized programming languages. Because it is a scripting language, Python is fast and efficient in aspects such as machine learning and automation.

Python offers a wide range of syntactical constructions, standard libraries, functions, and development features that are immensely helpful when working with elements such as statistical computations and data science.

Since its launch, python has dramatically improved, and its uses are as varied and as large-scale as application and software development.

In this book, we are going to cover a primary way of using python: *Data science.*

We will start by learning python basics, then move on to learning how to use it to read and analyze data from various sources, then clean and visualize the data, and finally, data wrangling and interpretation.

NOTE: If you have never programmed before, some aspects of this guidebook may prove challenging because the assumption made is that you have some Python programming experience.

Given the above, the section covering the basics of python will not be very detailed and may, therefore, lack some python programming aspects essential to understanding programming using the language, but that are non-integral to using python for data science.

Let us get started in earnest by looking at what data science is:

PS: I'd like your feedback. If you are happy with this book, please leave a review on Amazon.

Please leave a review for this book on Amazon by visiting the page below:

https://amzn.to/2VMR5qr

Your Gift

Let me help you master this and other programming stuff quickly.

Visit

https://bit.ly/codetutorials

To Find Out More

Table of Contents

Introduction _____ 2

Table of Contents _____ 5

Chapter 1: Introduction To Data Science ___ 8

Why Python For Data Science _____ 8

Chapter 2: Python Installation And Setup 11

How To Install Python On Windows _____ 11

How To Install Python On MacOS _____ 13

How To Install Python On Linux _____ 14

Required Python Libraries _____ 15

Chapter 3: Anaconda Environment Overview _____ 23

About Anaconda Virtual Environments _____ 27

Chapter 4: Python Programming Basics –A Refresher_____ 30

Python Logic_____ 30

Python Data Types_____ 33

Conditionals And Loops _____ 41

Python Functions_____ 44

Chapter 5: Data Analysis Using Numpy___ 47

Numpy Multidimensional Array Object _____ 48

Numpy ndarrays Data Types _____ 57

Numpy Array Attributes And Methods _____ 59

Numpy Arrays Indexing And Selection _____ 62

Numpy Arrays Operations _____ 65

Array Transpose & Axes Swap_____ 70

Chapter 6: Data Analysis Using Pandas___ 71

Introduction to Pandas Data Structures: Series And DataFrames _____ 72

Working With External Data Sources _____ *92*

Chapter 7: Data Wrangling _____ 95

Hierarchical Indexing _____ *95*

Dataset Merge & Combining Operations _____ *97*

Permutations and Random Sampling _____ *100*

Chapter 8: Data Visualization With Matplotlib _____ 101

Matplotlib _____ *101*

Pandas Built-In Visualization _____ *107*

Conclusion _____ 112

Chapter 1: Introduction To Data Science

We define data science as the comprehensive study of extensively large amounts of data to derive information and then use the derived information to make reliable decisions.

Data science uses logical procedures, mathematical algorithms, statistical patterns and processes to analyze the data and use it to arrive at logical decisions and plans. It mainly consists of mathematical statistics and scientific computations and helps in the extraction of information from the data sources such as structured and unstructured data.

This book covers how to perform data science using the Python programming language.

Why Python For Data Science

There're hundreds (over 700) of programming languages and each of them can work with data analysis when used by seasoned professionals. However, these languages are never primarily used for data science.

The reasons why Python is the most preferred programming language for data science and scientific computations are varied. The most standout of these factors include:

- **Simplicity:** To date, Python remains one of the simplest computer programming languages. One reason for this is because Python does not have a complex syntax, which in turn helps in data science processes that involve tons and tons of computations and analysis. Because of its syntax simplicity, Python lays a solid foundation for beginners to start working with data.

- **Architecture Neutral**: Python is architecture-neutral because it can run on any device. That means a Python-built program written on a Windows-based PC will run on a Linux--based distribution provided that it's not operating system dependent. This feature is of vital importance since after the creation of a program, you will not need to recreate the program from scratch should your development environment change.

- **Data source:** Python provides a simple and ideal environment for working with external data sources, including data sources such as logs, raw text files, relational databases such as SQL and spreadsheets using various libraries such as Pandas –discussed later. It also provides an ideal visual layout for data visualization.

- **Massive Libraries:** Python has many in-built tools and libraries for data science, which is one of its main advantages over languages such as R and others that, despite being efficient in data operations such as data cleaning and sorting, lack the tools available in python to perform operations such as machine learning and automation.

- **Powerful:** Over the years, Python has developed well to become a sort of Swiss Army knife of computer programming languages. It has powerful functions that are essential to machine learning algorithms and data analysis.

- **Open-source:** Python is open-source, and thus, its development never stops thanks to the army of open-sourced developers working on it at any given time. The programming language has a robust developer community support that provides regular updates.

Those are some of the advantages of using Python over other programming languages for data science.

Having looked at this, we can now move on to setting up our development environment:

Chapter 2: Python Installation And Setup

Python is very versatile, and different programmers use it for various applications. As such, you can set up Python and the required libraries in several ways based on your specific needs.

In this section, we are going to cover how to setup up Python for data science and statistical computation for various Operating systems. This book shall use the Free Anaconda Python distribution that comes pre-packaged with most of the libraries required for data science.

NOTE: For maximum compatibility with the code found in the book, we recommend using the latest version of Python, i.e., at the time of writing this, Python 3.8.

How To Install Python On Windows

To set up Anaconda on Windows, open the browser and navigate to the webpage below and select the latest version of the python —at the time of writing this book, version 3.7 is the most recent.

https://www.anaconda.com/downloads

Python For Data Analysis

Python 3.7 version

Download

64-Bit Graphical Installer (462 MB)
32-Bit Graphical Installer (410 MB)

Once you download the anaconda installer, follow the installation instructions. If you do not have any other version of Python on your computer, ensure you enable the option to add anaconda to PATH as shown in the figure below:

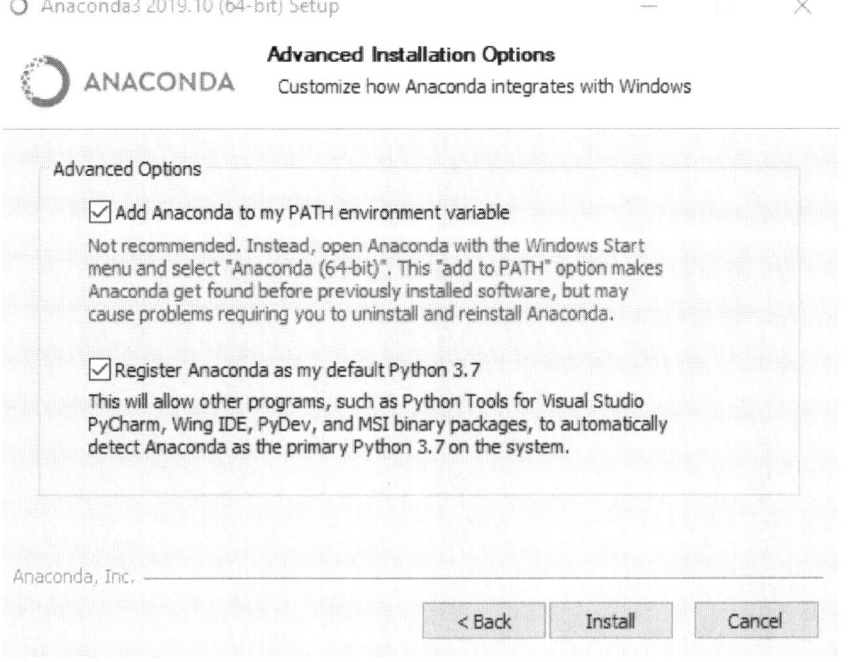

Once the installation is complete, verify that Python has installed correctly by launching the command prompt.

To open the command prompt, press the Windows key + R to launch the Run utility. Enter the command cmd.exe and press enter. Once the Cmd has started, enter the command Python to start the python interpreter and display the version of anaconda installed as shown below:

```
Python 3.7.4 (default, Aug  9 2019, 18:34:13) [MSC v.1915 64 bit (AMD64)] :: Anaconda, Inc. on win32
Type "help", "copyright", "credits" or "license" for more information.
>>>
```

You can exit the python interpreter by pressing CTRL + Z or entering the command exit().

How To Install Python On MacOS

To install anaconda on macOS, download the installation package from the web resource below, which should contain a name such as `Anaconda3-2019.10-MacOSX-x86_64.pkg`.

https://www.anaconda.com/download/#macos

Once downloading completes, launch the installer package and follow the installation instructions. Once the installation is complete, open your bash profile file to check whether the anaconda executable path is there (added). The profile is in /home/$USER/.bash_profile.

Open the terminal to test whether it is working correctly and enter the command python, which will launch the python interpreter and display the installed version of anaconda. You can exit by executing the command exit () or pressing Command + D

How To Install Python On Linux

Anaconda installation differs slightly on Linux-based distribution. For this section, we will cover the anaconda installation for Debian-based distributions. The installation is not dependent on Debian systems and can be used on any Linux distro

Navigate to the anaconda downloads page and download the Linux installation package, which should have a .sh extension. Once you have downloaded it, open the terminal and navigate to the folder where you stored the downloaded package. To navigate to the directory, enter the command `cd ~/Downloads`.

Once in the directory, make the anaconda installation package executable by executing the command `chmod 775 Anaconda2-2019.10-Linux-x86_64.sh`. Once the command completes, launch the anaconda installation script by entering the command `bash ./Anaconda2-2019.10-Linux-x86_64.sh`.

Once you read and accept the licenses, the anaconda installer will ask where to store your files. Ensure you install in a directory where you have read and write permissions. Using the default will store the files in /home/$USER/Anaconda.

Anaconda installation may require you to prepend the bin directory to your environment path variable, click yes to add the bin directory to the path. If you encounter problems while adding the path, edit the .bashrc, and enter the following line

export PATH=/home/$USER/anaconda3/bin:$PATH. Now save and close the file. Enter the command source .bashrc to update the path variables.

For some Linux distributions, you can install Python using the default package manager such as apt or pacman.

Required Python Libraries

If you are new to using Python for data science, you may have never heard of python libraries and its data ecosystem. We are going to look at a brief overview of the Python libraries used for data science.

NumPy

NumPy is a Python Linear Library used in scientific computing, machine learning, and data analysis. It comprises of multidimensional array objects and routines for processing arrays. NumPy, which stands for Numerical Python, is essential in data analysis using python.

NumPy provides the following operations:

- ndarrays: Fast and space-efficient array objects that represent multidimensional and homogenous items. ndarrays also includes arithmetic operations and classy broadcasting capabilities.

- Linear algebraic expressions and Fourier number translations.

- Integration with C and C++ code.

- Tools for working with memory-shaped files.

- Reads and writes arrays to and from disks.

- Provides fast and accurate mathematical functions without re-writing loops

NumPy does not provide high-level data analytics capabilities. Nevertheless, you must have a firm understanding of NumPy arrays array computing because having this knowledge helps build up other library knowledge such as Pandas which we shall discuss below and in a later section.

Data analysis mainly focuses on the following operations:

- Array operations for data cleaning, subsetting, filtering, and transformation

- Array algorithms such as sorting and set procedures

- Conditional logical array expressions

- Group data manipulation

- Relational data manipulation

- Data alignment

Outside the rapid data processing provided by NumPy arrays, NumPy arrays act as containers for data that is accessible by the developed algorithms and libraries.

Compared to Python data structures, NumPy arrays are more efficient for storing and manipulating statistical data. Because it can integrate well with other programming languages, Libraries written in other languages such as C++

or C can perform operations on the NumPy arrays without copying the data in other representations.

Pandas

Pandas is one of the most scientific and data computation libraries for Python. Pandas provide high-level functions and data structures used to work on structured data. The term 'Pandas' is a derivation of the words panel data, which is an econometrics term for multidimensional structured data. Pandas is a very dynamic and diverse library for working with real-world data.

In this book, we are going to focus on the Pandas DataFrame, which is a two-dimensional, column-based, tabular data structure with labeled rows and columns, and the Pandas Series, which is a one-dimensional array that is efficient for storing data types such as integers, strings, floats, and other python objects.

Pandas deliver sophisticated indexing functionalities that make it easy to perform operations such as reshaping, aggregation, dicing, and sub-selection on the data. Thanks to its flexibility, Pandas create a link between the high-performance, array-computation capabilities of NumPy and its flexible data manipulation capabilities such as working with external data sources like spreadsheets and relational databases. Pandas offer features such as:

- Flexibility in handling incorrect or missing data

- Time series functionality integrated into Pandas.

- Arithmetic operations preserving data source metadata

- A unique data structure to handle both non-time series time-series data

- Relational database operations such as merging, sorting, grouping, and more

- Labeled axes data structures that support automatic and explicit data alignment, which prevents errors that occur from using data sources with misaligned index.

Matplotlib

Matplotlib is a Python statistical plotting library that allows you to create visual representations of data such as graphs in two-dimensions. Initially created by John D. Hunter, Matplotlib now has a large team of developers that help maintain it.

By design, Matplotlib works well at creating plots suitable for publication and visual analysis of data. We have many visualization libraries available to Python programmers. However, Matplotlib is the most widely adopted primarily because it generally has good integrations with other Python data analytics libraries.

Matplotlib offers the same plotting capabilities as MATLAB such as providing full control over the figure plotted and flexibility. It also works efficiently with the Pandas DataFrame and NumPy Arrays. Matplotlib acts as a primary building block of other Python plotting libraries such as Seaborn, which we will cover in later sections.

Scikit-Learn

Scikit-learn is one of Python's machine learning library. This vast and efficient toolkit for machine learning encompasses modules for machine learning models such as:

- Clustering such as Hierarchical clustering, Fuzzy clustering, model-based clustering, spectral clustering, and k-means clustering.

- Model Selection: Cross validations, grid searches, metrics, Bayesian optimization, and Gradient-based optimization.

- Classification: Neural Networks, Random forests, decision trees, Support Vector Machines, Nearest Neighbors

- Regression: Linear regression, Logistic Regression, Stepwise regression, Lasso regression, Elastic Net regression, Ridge regression, and Polynomial regression

- Preprocessing: Aggregation, Sampling, Feature subset reduction, Normalization, variable transformation and Discretization, and Binarization.

- Dimensionality Reduction: Matrix factorization, PCA, Factor Analysis, Low variance filter, High correlation filter, and Backward feature elimination.

Developers have used Scikit-learn in conjunction with other libraries such as Pandas and statsmodel to produce high-performance algorithms. While we will not learn about machine learning algorithms or utilize the Scikit-learn toolkit, we might refer to it occasionally.

Statsmodel

Statsmodel is another Python library for data science widely used for statistical analysis. Statsmodel is a Python library used to perform statistical tests and implement various statistical models for extensive data exploration. Statsmodel was developed at Stanford University by Professor Jonathan Taylor. Compared with Scikit-learn, statsmodel has algorithms for classical statistics and econometrics.

They include submodules such as:

- Regression models such as linear mixed-effects models, robust linear models, generalized linear models and linear regression.

- Nonparametric methods such as Kernel density estimation and kernel regression.

- Analysis of variance.

- Time series analysis

- Visualization of statistical model results

You now know how to install Python and some of its primary libraries. We can move on:

Python For Data Analysis

Chapter 3: Anaconda Environment Overview

In this section, we are going to look at the most important features of the Python environment we set up in the previous section. You must understand how to use the Anaconda Navigator to get the best experience and troubleshoot any problems that may arise.

To start the Anaconda Navigator, Open the start menu and select Anaconda Navigator or use the terminal for Mac or Linux users. Once launched, a window similar to the one shown below will appear.

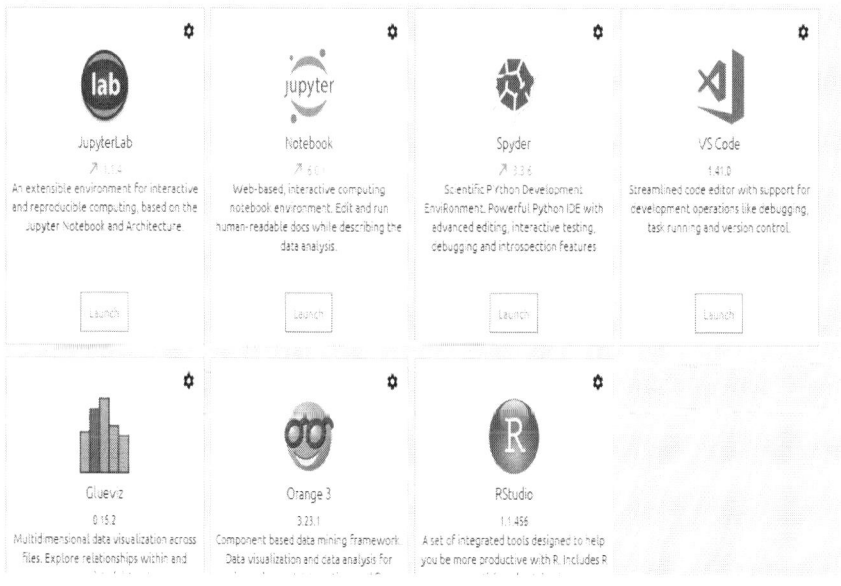

For this book, we are going to focus mostly on the Jupyter Notebook, which is an interactive scientific computation tool. Jupyter notebook provides a browser interface that you can use to write code and run it automatically.

To launch it, click the Launch button in anaconda navigator to start it up. You can also use the command prompt or terminal for Linux and Mac users. Once in the terminal, enter the command `jupyter notebook`, which will open the browser and redirect you to the jupyter notebook interface as shown below.

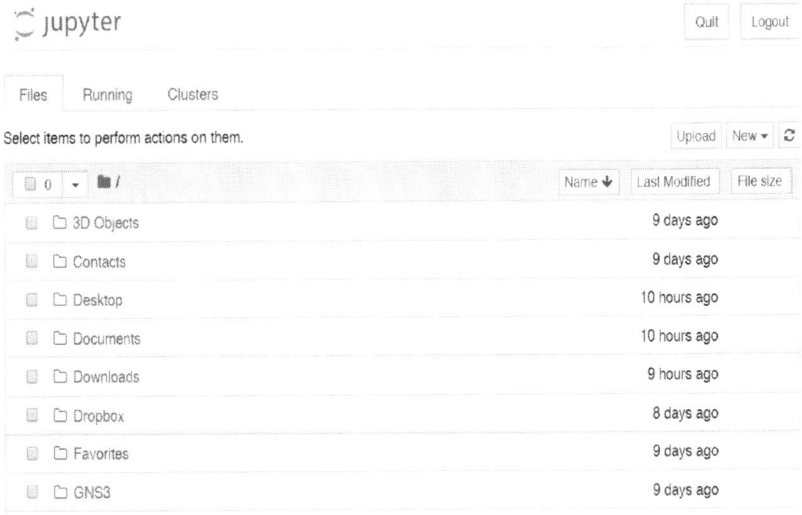

Jupyter notebook will open in the directory it was launched in so avoid launching it as root for Mac and Linux users or administrators for windows users. This refers to the

%windir% for windows user and the / directory for Linux and Mac users.

Now create a folder called Data-Science-2019; we shall use this folder to put all the programming code used in this book.

To create a new notebook, open the folder we created, and under new, select Python 3. Once a new window opens, enter the name of the file under the untitled section and click 'save.'

The box that opens is what we call a code cell. It allows you to enter Python code and then run it. For example: enter the code `print ("Hello world")`

Once you enter the code, you can run it by clicking SHIFT + RETURN. An output of the code will display and create a new code cell as illustrated below.

To create a new cell below the already executed cell, you can use the ALT + RETURN key to create it. To save the notebook after working on it, you can use the CTRL + S or select the floppy disk icon. Jupyter notebook also has an autosave feature that activates every two mins.

If you want to download the code from the notebook in various formats such as .py, .html, and .txt, you can click on the file menu, then download as, and select the file format you wish to download. Some formats may require the installation of various packages.

If you encounter a code that is running forever, perhaps a code error or so, the cell with the code running will have an asterisk. To interrupt the execution, look at the top bar, select Kernel, and then select Restart kernel. To get more information on Jupyter notebook in general and other libraries from the Anaconda distribution, you can use the help option found at the top menu.

About Anaconda Virtual Environments

This advanced subsection covers how to create anaconda virtual environments. We use Anaconda virtual environments to set up Python and various selected libraries as separate environments to avoid messing up the base environment.

For example, if you have a default Anaconda Python 3 installation, you can create a virtual environment that runs Python 2 without affecting the other installation. You can also install libraries on the virtual environment, activate, deactivate, and delete it whenever necessary.

Instances of where you may need to create a virtual environment include:

- When you create a python program that runs on a particular version of a library

- Upon the release of a new version of the library you used

- You want to test out the code using the latest release and do not want the previous code to break. In this case, you can create a virtual environment with the newest version and test it out without affecting the older code.

To find out more about virtual environments using the anaconda distribution, navigate to the following resource page

https://conda.io/projects/conda/en/latest/user-guide/concepts/environments.html

Launch the command prompt to start creating virtual environments. As stated earlier, do not open the command prompt as admin as it will create the virtual environments in the `%systemroot%system32` directory. Once you launch the command prompt, enter the following command `conda create - -name VirtualEnviron Matplotlib`.

The above code creates a virtual environment called VirtualEnviron and associates the Matplotlib library with it. Anaconda gets the package metadata and all the required libraries and installs them in the specified environment. Activate the created environment, using the command `conda activate VirtualEnviron`. To deactivate the environment, use the command `conda deactivate VirtualEnviron`.

We can test the difference between this environment and the base Python environment by importing modules not installed in the environment. For example, the VirtualEnviron environment created was using the Matplotlib library. If we try to import a package that does not exist such as Pandas, it will result in an error.

```
C:\Users\Captain salem>conda activate VirtualEnviron

(VirtualEnviron) C:\Users\Captain salem>python
Python 3.7.5 (default, Oct 31 2019, 15:18:51) [MSC v.1916 64 bit (AMD64)] :: Anaconda, Inc. on win32
Type "help", "copyright", "credits" or "license" for more information.
>>> import pandas as pd
Traceback (most recent call last):
  File "<stdin>", line 1, in <module>
ModuleNotFoundError: No module named 'pandas'
```

This happens because the virtual environment VirtualEnviron does not have the panda's library installed. To install it on the virtual environment, you can use the `conda install Pandas` command.

To create an environment with a different version of python, you can use the command `conda create -name AnotherVersion python=3.6 zipline`, which creates a virtual environment running python 3.6 with the zipline library as specified.

To use Python for data science, you need to understand the fundamentals of the python programming language. In the next section, we are going to cover the basics of python to get you up and running as a data scientist.

Chapter 4: Python Programming Basics —A Refresher

The first part of this section is going to cover the basics of Python programming and then we shall move on to more essential Python concepts such as Functions, data structures, and other built-in tools for data science.

Python Logic

One feature that makes Python a great language is its simplicity. Because of its simplicity, we mainly refer to is as an executable pseudocode. Let us tackle some of the semantics that accompanies this excellent programming language.

Indentation

Unlike other major programming languages such as Java, C++, C, R, and Perl that uses curly braces to structure the code, Python uses indentation (whitespaces – tabs and space) to structure the code. The code below shows the structure of a loop in Python and Java.

```python
for syllables in "python for data science":
    if syllables == 'a' or syllables == 's':
            continue
    print('Current syllable is :', syllables)
    var = 10
```

Structure of a loop in Python

```java
public class Main
{
  public static void main (String[]args)
  {
    for (int i = 0; i < 10; i++)
      {
    System.out.println ("Python For Data science");
      }
  }
}
```

Structure of a loop in Java

In the first example program —written in Python—, we see that the program does not require curly braces to structure the program. All you need is to indent the code at the same level. A colon indicates the start of an indented code block, after which you must indent all the code by the same amount until the end of the block. Depending on development environment —most of them will insert indentation automatically— use tabs to insert blocks.

In the second Java program, we can see that it requires the use of curly braces to enclose the section of the loop. Moreover, we can see that in Java, statement termination with semicolons is necessary while in python, it's not, which is definite proof that Python offers simple syntax compared to other languages.

Object Model Consistency

Python is most famous for its object model consistency. All data structures in Python are *a python object*. Python interprets every string, number, list, function, class, or module as objects with its internal data and type, which offers vast flexibility over other programming languages that may lack the same feature.

Python Comments

Documenting python code is very easy using the # sign (octothorpe) for single-line comments. Comments also come in handy when testing a particular block of code without having to delete the previous code. For example:

```
import math
my_list = [12,-15,22,35,-10,17.8, 45,33]

# for i in my_list:
#     print(i)
def area(radius):
    return math.pi * radius ** 2
area(42)
```

You can also insert comments after a block of code – we usually use this to explain a single line of code.

```
print("Hello world") # explains one line
```

Python Data Types

Python has the following data types:

Numbers

Numbers are a type of data type used to store numeric values only. Python supports three types of numbers. They include floats, integers, and complex numbers.

Unlike some programming languages where you declare the variable data type before using it, Python requires you to only declare the name of the variable, and then the equal sign and the assigned value.

```
age = 22
```

Floats

We use floats, also called real-numbers, to represent decimal numbers, and we frequently represent them with a decimal point. In Python, we can also represent floats in scientific notation using the exponential symbol. Example: `0.84e5 = 84000.0`

Integers

In Python, we use Integers to represent 'whole' numerical values that do not have decimal points. Integers can be either positive or negative representation.

```
x = 10
y = -34
type(x)
type(y)
```

```
int
```

Complex Numbers

In python, we represent Complex numbers as x + yi where x and y represent float numbers, and i equals the square root of -1 (imaginary number). Complex numbers are not very common in Python programming but the language does support them.

Long

Long, also called long integers, are integers of unlimited size. We write them as integers followed by uppercase or lowercase L. Only Python2 supports this type of numbers.

To find the type of a variable, use the type() method built into python

Python Mathematical Functions

Python has the following built-in mathematical functions that help complete mathematical calculations.

- abs(y) – returns the absolute value of a given number.

- exp(y) – returns exponential of y.

- log(y) – return the natural logarithm of y.

- log10(y) – returns the logarithm of y to base 10.

- mix(x, y,) – returns the minimum value of the provided arguments.

- max(x, y,...) – returns the maximum value of the provided arguments.

- sqrt(y) – returns the square root of y.

Trigonometric Functions

Python supports trigonometric functions to perform trigonometric operations. They include:

- sin(value) – returns the sine of a given value in radians.

- tan(value) – returns the tangent of a given value in radians.

- degrees(value) – converts radians to degrees of the specified angle.

- cos(value) – returns the cosine of a given value in radians.

- asin(value) – returns the arc sine of a given value in radians

Mathematical Constants

Used to define the common mathematical constants, mathematical constants include:

- math.pi – mathematical constant π = 3.1415

- math.e - mathematical constant e = 2.7182

Random Number Functions

We use Random functions to generate random numbers and perform operations in a data type. They mainly apply in games, simulation, and cipher, and other security applications. They include:

- random() – a random whole number x. i.e., 0 is less than or equal to x and x is less than 1.

- shuffle(lst) – used to randomly reshuffle items in a list in place.

Strings

Strings are amongst the most commonly used data type in Python. A string is a sequence of ordered characters. To represent a string in Python, we enclose the characters with single or double-quotes. We use triple quotes to enclose multiple lines of characters such as paragraphs. Strings are immutable; thus, once you declare a Python string, you cannot update its contents. Unlike other programming languages, Python does not support character type.

String Concatenation

String concatenation refers to a method of adding two or more Python strings to form one complete string. For example:

```
In [2]: "hello" + " world"
        'hello world'
In [4]: string1 = "Hello"
        string2 = " world"
        string1 + string2
        'Hello world'
In [ ]:
```

String Repetition

In Python, String repetition refers to the operation of repeating a series of characters the number of times specified.

String Slicing

Slicing is a method of extracting parts of a string. We accomplish this using python string indexing. Python is a zero-based index language; thus, the first set of a string is position zero forward. Python also supports negative indexing.

Lists

Lists are types of data that act as containers that store multiple data types in a single and unique container. We create a Python list using the square brackets. Data in a list can be an integer, float, string, a nested list, or a Python dictionary. Since they contain mutable elements within, this makes Python lists mutable. Items in a list correspond to an index that starts at index 0.

To add details to an existing list, we use the .append() method. To delete elements in a list, you can use the del method if you are sure of which index you want to remove, or if not, the remove() method.

List Operations

Operations such as concatenation and repletion that work on strings can work on Python lists. You can concatenate lists using the + and repeat them using the *. However, the result, in this case, is another string. You can carry out all string operations on Lists as well.

The following are some of the operations carried out on a string and list

- Indexing
- Slicing
- Sequencing

Tuples

In Python, a tuple is a sequence of immutable Python objects. Tuples are sequences of Python data. We create tuples using parenthesis; this is very much unlike lists that we create using square brackets and are immutable, i.e. cannot be changed or updated. Lists are mutable.

You can create a python tuple by typing two parentheses with nothing in it to create an empty tuple. Similar operations such as indexing and concatenation apply to tuples too in the same way they apply to lists and strings.

To access an element in a tuple, we use a square bracket followed by the index of the element you would like to access. You cannot change Tuples as they are immutable, which means you cannot update or change the elements in a tuple.

Sets

A set is an iterable, mutable, and unordered collection of data types. We create a set by separating items in braces {}. Sets cannot contain duplicate items; they support operations such as intersections and unions. Since Sets is an unordered collection of data, it does not support slicing.

Booleans

Boolean operators are Python data types that are either true or false. Based on the condition, they evaluate to either true or false.

Dictionaries

Dictionaries are the most common type of data for complex programs, which is because dictionaries are the most flexible data type available in Python. In Python, we use Dictionaries to store vast amounts of data. In Python, we use curly braces {} to define dictionaries.

Dictionaries use keys as identifiers for specific groups of data within it. We then use the key to retrieve the corresponding data and not vice versa. The basic syntax for dictionaries is:

`{key:value, key:value, key:value}`

Dictionaries can contain any data types such as strings, numbers, and even nested dictionaries.

Conditionals And Loops

Loops and conditionals are fundamental programming constructs that make programs more engaging. Conditional and Loops can be complex or simple depending on the usage and the formatting. Python features numerous built-in keywords for conditional logic, loops, and other standard control flow concepts found in other programming languages. The following are the primary conditionals and loops keywords.

If, Elif, else

The if statement is the most commonly used control flow statement in Python and other major programming languages. It checks for a condition and executes the preceding block of code if it's true.

A set of Elif statements can follow the if statement to check for multiple conditions based on specified criteria. If all the conditions on upper blocks evaluate to false, we use an else statement that executes in place of the missing true Boolean results from the upper conditional statements.

If a condition evaluates to true, the preceding Elif or else blocks will not execute and the program will automatically exit out of the condition block.

Loops

Loops also play a significant role in program execution. Loops may appear similar to conditional statements such as if...else statement but differ in mode of operation.

Unlike conditionals, Loops will run a block of code repeatedly as long as the condition is true. They, however, rely on conditional statements for execution. We have two main types of Python loops.

For loop

In Python, we use the for loop to run a block of code until the condition becomes false. We usually use the for loop when we have an unknown number of iterations.

For loops can be advanced over to the next iteration by use of the continue keyword, which causes the loop to skip the current block and continue to the next block of code. To break a for loop out of flow, we use the break keyword, which terminates the current flow of the inner loop and exits to the outer block of code.

While loop

A While loop has a condition and a block of code that will continue to run until the condition evaluates to false or loop is terminated with a break keyword. A while loop checks the condition first, then executes the code. We usually use this when we have an unknown and undefined number of iterations.

Nested Loop

Just like decision statements, you can have loops nested within each other. Loop nesting can be either a for loop inside a while loop, a while loop inside a while loop, or vice versa.

You should exercise caution while working with nested loops as they may cause the code to break or produce logically incorrect values.

Python Functions

When it comes to code reuse and organization in programming, Functions, also called methods in other programming languages, are essential.

We use Functions when we want to use the same block of code repeatedly. Instead of re-writing the code many times over, you can create a function and only call the function when needed. Functions also help organize the code and making it more readable.

To declare a Python function, we use the def keyword followed by the function name, function parameters inside the parenthesis. We also use the keyword return to ensure that the result from the function passes to the caller.

You can have more than one return statement with a function. If a function does not have a return statement, Python will automatically return a None value.

Python functions can have positional and keyword arguments. We use keyword arguments or parameters to specify default or placeholder values. Placeholder values are optional —this means that one can choose to pass them during function call or not with no errors. However, arguments in a python function must follow positional arguments. The best way to avoid error is to use a keyword for the required arguments. For example:

```
def area(length=10, width=20):
    return length * width
area(length=30, width=60)
```

Once you assign a keyword variable, you can pass the arguments in any preferred order as long as the variable corresponds.

Function Scope

In Python, functions can access variables in two scopes. Think of scope as jurisdiction over the variables within a program. The two variable scopes in Python are the *global scope* and the *local scope*.

By default, Python assigns the local scope tag to variables declared inside a function, and thus, other functions can access the variables inside another function unless explicitly specified. Local scope, also called local namespace, is created upon function call and destroyed once the function has completed executing.

There are some exceptions not covered in the book. Passing variables outside of the function's scope is probable, but you must state these variables as global using the global keyword.

NOTE: The above section does not cover any detailed Python Programming. It only acts as a brief overview to refresh your Python knowledge. Before proceeding into further sections, make sure you have a solid understanding of Python programming.

Chapter 5: Data Analysis Using Numpy

Numpy, short for Numerical Python, is one of the most foundational packages for numerical computing in Python. Numpy is a Python linear algebra library that offers scientific computing functionalities using Numpy arrays.

As we discussed earlier, Numpy has substantial flexibility and features including integration with other programming languages. Numpy itself does not provide extensive scientific functionalities, but it lays a foundation for understanding other libraries in the PyData Ecosystem such as Pandas, and is therefore a building block for other libraries. Numpy is designed with efficiency in mind and working with large arrays of data.

To install Numpy on your computer, we recommend using the Anaconda distribution for this. If you are using other packages of Python, you can install it by running pip or conda using the commands:

```
pip install Numpy
```

```
conda install Numpy
```

Numpy Multidimensional Array Object

The key feature of Numpy is the N-dimensional array object also called ndarrays. The Numpy array is a flexible container that is efficient and fast for storing large datasets in Python.

These Numpy arrays allow one to perform mathematical calculations on a large scalar data between scalar elements. To create a Numpy array, launch jupyter notebook and create a new notebook called Numpy. Start by importing Numpy the conventional way using the command

import Numpy as np

```
import numpy as np
```

This command imports the Numpy package and assigns it the name np. Next, we can create a Numpy array by generating random data or from native Python data types such as Lists and tuples, which accepts any sequence-like object and then produces a new Numpy array that contains the passed data, as shown below:

```
In [8]: my_list = [70,45,34,223,453,62,45,-34,334,87]

In [10]: np.array(my_list) # create an array from list
Out[10]: array([ 70,  45,  34, 223, 453,  62,  45, -34, 334,  87])
```

To generate random data using Numpy, use the code shown below:

```
In [11]: my_array = np.random.randn(4,6) # create array from random data

In [12]: my_array
Out[12]: array([[-0.8897291 ,  1.75725262, -0.90983441, -2.08354029,  0.08807145,
          1.28412815],
        [ 0.35220844, -0.17922757,  0.1680843 ,  0.19151129, -0.49345795,
          0.16096518],
        [-0.12355841, -0.56511338, -1.36351546,  0.15445353,  0.09864299,
         -0.50692708],
        [ 1.03267357,  0.76723545,  0.69264177,  0.22063241,  1.00967844,
          1.24743555]])
```

A Numpy array is a generic multidimensional container meant for use on homogeneous data i.e. all elements ought to be of the same type. Each array has a shape, which is a tuple indicating the size of each dimension, and a dtype, which is an object describing the data type of the array:

Nested Python lists of equal length convert into a multidimensional array once passed to the Numpy array() function. To find out the shape of an array, we use the .shape() function.

```
In [27]: list_ = [[1,2,3,4],[5,6,7,8]]

In [30]: array2 = np.array(list_)

In [34]: array2
Out[34]: array([[1, 2, 3, 4],
        [5, 6, 7, 8]])
```

The above code produces a two-dimensional array with two rows and four columns that we can identify by looking at the number of square brackets of the array.

The best and fastest way to create Numpy arrays is by using the Numpy built-in random data generating functions. One of them is randon.randn shown above.

The most common built-in Numpy function for generating random data is the arrange() function. The Numpy arrange function is similar to the python arange function. In the arange function, we pass the start, step and step size to generate evenly spaced values within the given interval.

For example:

```
np.arange(0,20,2)
```

```
array([ 0,  2,  4,  6,  8, 10, 12, 14, 16, 18])
```

In the above example, we create an array of even numbers between 0 to but not including 20, which creates a single-dimensional array of 10 elements. The arange function comes in handy when you require quick random data for testing.

Another useful Numpy functions for generating quick data is np.zeros() function. This function creates an array of given shape and type filled with pure zeros. It accepts three parameters: shape, dtype, and order. For example:

```
In [12]: np.zeros((5,5))
Out[12]: array([[0., 0., 0., 0., 0.],
                [0., 0., 0., 0., 0.],
                [0., 0., 0., 0., 0.],
                [0., 0., 0., 0., 0.],
                [0., 0., 0., 0., 0.]])
```

Once you pass the arguments as a tuple, the first argument will represent the number of rows, and the second number represents the number of columns.

To get an array of ones only, you can use the np.ones() function to accomplish this. Similar to the .zeros() function, you can have a single number to create a single-dimensional array or a tuple to create a multi-dimensional array.

```
In [13]: np.ones((3,5))
Out[13]: array([[1., 1., 1., 1., 1.],
                [1., 1., 1., 1., 1.],
                [1., 1., 1., 1., 1.]])
```

Linspace is another Numpy built-in function that allows you to create an array of evenly spaced random numbers over a specified interval. Despite the small similarity, do not confuse linspace with arange. The arange function takes the third argument as the step size while linspace will take the third argument as the number of points you want.

```
In [16]: np.linspace(5,10,50)
Out[16]: array([ 5.        ,  5.10204082,  5.20408163,  5.30612245,  5.40816327,
         5.51020408,  5.6122449 ,  5.71428571,  5.81632653,  5.91836735,
         6.02040816,  6.12244898,  6.2244898 ,  6.32653061,  6.42857143,
         6.53061224,  6.63265306,  6.73469388,  6.83673469,  6.93877551,
         7.04081633,  7.14285714,  7.24489796,  7.34693878,  7.44897959,
         7.55102041,  7.65306122,  7.75510204,  7.85714286,  7.95918367,
         8.06122449,  8.16326531,  8.26530612,  8.36734694,  8.46938776,
         8.57142857,  8.67346939,  8.7755102 ,  8.87755102,  8.97959184,
         9.08163265,  9.18367347,  9.28571429,  9.3877551 ,  9.48979592,
         9.59183673,  9.69387755,  9.79591837,  9.89795918, 10.        ])
```

The above code creates a one-dimensional array random data between 5 and 10 containing 50 data points. While this may look like a two-dimensional array, it is a one-dimensional array which is illustrated by the number of square brackets before the array values.

You can also use Numpy to create an identity matrix – an identity matrix is a square matrix – where the number of columns equals the number of rows –in which all the elements of the principal diagonal are ones and all other elements are zeros. This is very handy while dealing with linear algebraic problems.

Python For Data Analysis

To create this kind of matrix in Numpy, we use the .eye() function and pass a number to represent the number of rows and columns.

```
In [19]: np.eye(5)

Out[19]: array([[1., 0., 0., 0., 0.],
                [0., 1., 0., 0., 0.],
                [0., 0., 1., 0., 0.],
                [0., 0., 0., 1., 0.],
                [0., 0., 0., 0., 1.]])
```

Let us discuss the np.random methods in Numpy that allow us to create arrays of random data. There is a wide range of these functions. For the sake of simplicity, we will only cover the most useful and common ones.

The first function is np.random.rand, which creates an array of the given shape and populates it with random sample data of a uniform distribution between zero and one.

```
In [9]: np.random.rand(5,5)
Out[9]: array([[1.84716445e-01, 1.87244935e-01, 1.02005755e-01, 6.77990893e-01,
         5.15857859e-01],
        [3.50562723e-01, 6.92747842e-04, 6.38287467e-01, 1.25202438e-01,
         3.88474143e-01],
        [5.32290502e-01, 3.67569200e-01, 3.17824478e-01, 2.68476198e-01,
         9.75629284e-01],
        [2.75155801e-01, 7.28588796e-02, 5.67418145e-01, 4.76902001e-01,
         2.35029304e-01],
        [7.38402775e-03, 8.94200608e-01, 6.66957236e-01, 9.90884004e-01,
         3.37352877e-01]])
```

From the example above, we can see that the rand function accepts two arguments natively unlike previous functions where we passed the arguments as tuples.

We can also generate an array that contains random values from a Gaussian distribution using the np.random.randn() function. Unlike rand, randn values are sampled around zero rather than zero and one.

```
In [11]: np.random.randn(5,5)
Out[11]: array([[-0.48467658, -1.02733662,  2.5420179 , -2.2455603 , -0.59912718],
        [-1.22515728,  0.38957422, -1.06403899, -0.1148138 , -0.66081275],
        [ 0.35599036, -0.44028795,  0.71652606, -0.18312592, -0.34281333],
        [ 1.00000367,  0.27691187,  2.50995267,  1.6960975 ,  0.88862582],
        [ 0.61111813,  2.03609034, -0.30130308, -0.43626406,  1.38013316]])
```

The other Numpy random generator function commonly used is the np.random.randint() . This function returns an array of random integers from a low to a high numerical value. It accepts three main arguments as low, high and step respectively.

Low value is inclusive while the high value is exclusive, which means that the low has a high probability of being generated compared to the high value with a low probability.

```
In [13]: np.random.randint(3,45,10)
Out[13]: array([17, 16,  7, 12,  3, 29, 20, 10, 38, 38])
```

The code above generates 10 random integers between 3 and 45 with 3 being inclusive (it appears in index 2) and 45 being exclusive.

The table below shows the standard Numpy functions. Numpy focuses on numerical computing, and if you are working with unspecified data, you should use float64 data type.

Function Name	Description
array	This function converts the specified data such as lists, dictionaries, tuples, etc into Numpy ndarray type. By default, it copies the data inside the specified type.

asarray	This function converts the specified data type to a Numpy ndarrays. it does not copy if the specified data type is already a Numpy ndarray
arange	This function acts as the default python range function. However, it returns a Numpy array type instead of a list
zeros	This function returns a Numpy array of all 0s with the given shape and dtype.
ones	This function returns a Numpy array of all 1s with the given shape and dtype.
Zeros_like	This function converts an array filled with 0s with the same shape and dtype.
Ones_like	This function converts an array filled with 1s with the same shape and dtype.
empty	This function creates an empty array by allocating new memory. It creates an empty array by not populating it with values.
full	This function returns a Numpy array of the given shape and dtype with all values set to the indicated value.

| Eye, identity | This function creates a N x N identity matrix |
| Full_like | This function acts as full upon an existing array. |

Numpy ndarrays Data Types

The data type of the array, mostly denoted as dtype in the documentation, is a special object type that contains the metadata related to its corresponding data.

The dtype is required by the ndarray to interpret a memory chunk as a specific data type. These are the basis of Numpy flexibility when interacting with data from other systems as they provide a direct mapping onto an underlying memory representation. It makes it easy to read and write binary data streams to and from disk and connect with low-level languages such as C. The dtypes are named conventionally followed by a numerical value indicating the number of bits per element.

Do not memorize the Numpy dtypes. You should only concentrate on the actual type of data you are working with; the following are the common dtypes of the Numpy ndarrays.

- Int8, uint8

- Int16, uint16

- Int32, unint32

- Int64, uint64

- Float16

- Float32

- Float64

- Float128

- Bool

- Object

- String_

- Unicode_

- Complex64

- Complex128

- Complex256

You can explicitly convert an array from one type to another using ndarray's astype method:

Numpy Array Attributes And Methods

Now let us take a look at Numpy array functions and methods. Let us start by creating an array object called my_array and use the arange function to generate sample data of 30 data points.

```
In [17]: my_array = np.arange(30)

In [18]: my_array
Out[18]: array([ 0,  1,  2,  3,  4,  5,  6,  7,  8,  9, 10, 11, 12, 13, 14, 15, 16,
               17, 18, 19, 20, 21, 22, 23, 24, 25, 26, 27, 28, 29])
```

We can also use the random.randint to generate 10 random values between 20 and 100 as shown below:

```
In [19]: random_values = np.random.randint(20,100,10)

In [20]: random_values
Out[20]: array([53, 91, 55, 80, 66, 80, 71, 87, 56, 82])
```

One of the most common methods you can perform on a Numpy array is the reshape method. It returns an array containing the same data with a different shape. For example:

```
In [22]: my_array.reshape(6,5)
Out[22]: array([[ 0,  1,  2,  3,  4],
                [ 5,  6,  7,  8,  9],
                [10, 11, 12, 13, 14],
                [15, 16, 17, 18, 19],
                [20, 21, 22, 23, 24],
                [25, 26, 27, 28, 29]])
```

The above returns the array with the specified number of rows (5) and the specified number of columns (6). Keep in mind that Numpy will give you an error if it is impossible to reshape the specified array correctly, which means the items in the array are impossible to fill in using the shape specified. For example, the array my_array contains 30 elements; if you try to reshape it into 5 by 5 matrix, you will get an error as shown:

```
In [23]: my_array.reshape(5,5)
---------------------------------------------------------------
ValueError                        Traceback (most recent call last)
<ipython-input-23-d6f47fce6ee2> in <module>
----> 1 my_array.reshape(5,5)

ValueError: cannot reshape array of size 30 into shape (5,5)
```

The best way to check if the specified shape is valid is to check whether the multiple of the shape equals the number of elements in the array. For example, 6x5 equals 30 and thus, an array with 30 elements will reshape correctly.

You can also find out the maximum and minimum value of the array using the min and max method.

```
In [26]: random_values.max()
Out[26]: 91
```

The above returns the maximum value within the specified array, which is also similar to the min function off the array. In some cases, we may not require the exact value of a maximum or minimum element in the array and may instead be interested in the index of these values. In such instances, we can use the argmax() or argmin() to get the index location of the maximum or minimum value.

```
In [28]: random_values.argmin()
Out[28]: 0
```

A useful attribute we can call off the Numpy array is the dtype, which returns the actual data type of the array.

```
In [29]: random_values.dtype
Out[29]: dtype('int32')
```

Numpy Arrays Indexing And Selection

This subsection will cover how to select elements or groups of elements from a Numpy array.

Launch the jupyter notebook and create a new notebook, import Numpy as np, and we can get started.

We will start by creating an array using the arrange function that contains 15 elements between 20 and 30.

```
In [2]: my_array = np.arange(20,30)

In [3]: my_array
Out[3]: array([20, 21, 22, 23, 24, 25, 26, 27, 28, 29])
```

In a Numpy array, elements are accessible through indexing and slicing just like any other Python container object. Indexing a Numpy array starts at index zero upward.

In Python, indexing methods are field index, basic slice, and advanced index. Similar to the basic Python indexing techniques, we use square brackets and the index notations to slice elements in a python object.

We can get the element at index 5 by passing the array name followed by index number inside square brackets

```
In [4]: my_array[5]
Out[4]: 25
```

To get elements in a range, we can specify the starting and the ending index to get the elements in that range. For example:

```
In [6]: my_array[2:6]
Out[6]: array([22, 23, 24, 25])
```

We can also fetch elements within a specific range using indexing. We pass the start and end index as shown:

```
In [5]: my_array[:8]
Out[5]: array([20, 21, 22, 23, 24, 25, 26, 27])
```

In this case, it returns the values from the first index (index 0) to index 8. To get a range of values, you pass the start and ending index. This prints the value from the start index to but not including the last index

```
In [6]: my_array[1:8]
Out[6]: array([21, 22, 23, 24, 25, 26, 27])
```

Another important part of Numpy array operation is slicing. We can create a variable that contains a slice of a certain array as shown:

```
In [8]: array_slice = my_array[:8]
```

```
In [9]: array_slice
Out[9]: array([20, 21, 22, 23, 24, 25, 26, 27])
```

The above array contains a slice of the main array with 8 elements. We can update the values in the array by broadcasting a single value in the array.

Upon broadcast, the array now contains 8, 67 elements. Since the array array_slice is part of the main array, if we call the main array, it will contain the broadcasted values.

```
In [10]: array_slice[:] = 67
```

```
In [11]: array_slice
Out[11]: array([67, 67, 67, 67, 67, 67, 67, 67])
```

This is because array slicing does not copy the data from the sliced array to the new array but instead contains a view of the full array. Numpy does this to avoid memory problems when working with a huge array.

```
In [12]: my_array
Out[12]: array([67, 67, 67, 67, 67, 67, 67, 67, 28, 29])
```

To copy a specific slice of the array, we use the .copy() method off the slice we would like to copy.

```
In [13]: array_slice = my_array.copy()
In [14]: array_slice
Out[14]: array([67, 67, 67, 67, 67, 67, 67, 67, 28, 29])
```

Now if we try to broadcast a value in the copied array, it will not affect the original array; only the copied values.

Numpy Arrays Operations

Similar to other Python data types, Numpy arrays allow us to perform various operations off of them. Although these operations may differ from native Python data types, the mode of operation may appear similar. The following are the supported Numpy array operations.

- Arithmetic Operations

- Logical Operations

- Conditional Expressional operations

Arithmetic Operations

Numpy arrays allow for basic arithmetic operations such as additions, subtractions, multiplication, division, modulus, and more. However, if you add arrays with a different number of elements and similar dimensions, Python will return an error.

```
-------------------------------------------------------------------
---
ValueError                          Traceback (most recent call la
st)
<ipython-input-17-8dd6b53bc5a6> in <module>
      1 var1 = np.array([19,20,23,24,25,27])
      2 var2 = np.array([10,11,12,13,14,15,34])
----> 3 var3 = var1 * var2

ValueError: operands could not be broadcast together with shapes (6,)
(7,)
```

The result is an array of the same dimension.

Arithmetic operations with scalar value return an array with each action performed on each array element.

```
In [15]: var1 = np.array([19,20,23,24,25,27])
         var2 = np.array([10,11,12,13,14,15])
         var3 = var1 * var2

In [16]: var3
Out[16]: array([190, 220, 276, 312, 350, 405])
```

These operations also apply to multi-dimensional arrays. The table below shows some standard functions supported by Numpy arrays:

Function Name	Function Description
Abs, fabs	
sqrt	
square	
exp	Returns an array with an exponent of each array element.
Log10, log Log2, log1p	Returns an array of natural logarithm log (e), log base 10, log base 2 and log (1 + x) in respective order.
ceil	Returns the array with the ceiling of each array element. Ceil is the smallest value that is greater than or equal to that value
floot	Returns the floor of each element in the array —The floor is the largest numerical value that is less than or equal to that value.
rint	Returns an array with each element

	rounded to the nearest integer while preserving the default data type.
modf	Return fractional and integral parts of an array as a separate array
sign	returns the sign of each element: 1 (positive), 0 (zero), or −1 (negative)
isfinite	Return boolean array that shows whether every element is finite (non-inf, non-NaN
Trigonometric functions – cos, sin, tan cosh, sinh, tanh	Regular and hyperbolic trigonometric functions
arccos, arcsin, arctan, arccosh, arcsinh, arctanh	Inverse trigonometric functions
sum	Sums all the values in the array of along a specified axis
cumprod	Returns the cumulative product of the array elements starting from 1

cumsum	Returns the cumulative sum of the array elements starting from 0
std	Returns the standard deviation with optional degrees of freedom adjustments
var	Returns the variance of the elements —like the standard deviation method
mean	Returns the arithmetic means of the elements in the array

NOTE: Those are some of the functions that can apply to an array. You can find more functions in the Numpy official documentation.

https://Numpy.org/doc/

Conditional Expression

You can use python conditional statements to search the values matching specified conditions. The return value of the conditional check on Numpy array is an array of Boolean values.

You can also pass an array of Booleans to an array to return the values matching the condition.

Logical Operations

Numpy provides logical operators such as logical_or and logical_and. Logical operators used in basic Python data types apply to Numpy arrays. You can find more information about Numpy operations here:

http://scipy-lectures.org/intro/Numpy/operations.html

Array Transpose & Axes Swap

Array Transpose refers to a special method of reshaping arrays. Transposing returns a view of the underlying data in the array without copying the values. An example of this is the broadcasting technique.

Among the methods supported by array, the transpose method is beneficial when requiring a view of the entire data set. Arrays also support the T attribute that swaps the axes of the array. You can also use the swapaxes method to perform this task.

You can find more information about Numpy array transpose here:

https://docs.scipy.org/doc/Numpy/reference/generated/Numpy.transpose.html

Chapter 6: Data Analysis Using Pandas

Now that we have briefly worked with Numpy, we can move on to working with Pandas —mainly built on Numpy. Pandas play a significant role in the data science process.

As mentioned in earlier sections, Pandas contains vast tools and data structures. It helps in data manipulation operations such as data cleaning and analysis in Python. We usually use it with other Numerical computing libraries such as Numpy or Scipy, Statsmodel, scikit-learn, Matplotlib, seaborn, and more.

Since it works of Numpy, Pandas implements substantial features of Numpy such as array-based computing functions. However, its development is such that it works with homogenous numerical array data in tabular formats.

We will be importing Pandas the conventional way using code.

Import Pandas as pd and thus, when you see pd in the code, it is referencing the Pandas package.

Introduction to Pandas Data Structures: Series And DataFrames

To master Pandas, we must build a solid foundation of its two main building blocks, i.e. DataFrames an21d Pandas Series. On their own, they do not provide a general solution while working with large amounts of data, but they offer a compact ground for most applications.

Pandas Series

A Pandas series refers to a one-dimensional array-like object that contains a series of values —similar to a Numpy array and an associated array of labels called an index. We can create the simplest Pandas series using a Numpy array as shown below:

```
In [2]: array = np.arange(0,20)

In [3]: series = pd.Series(array)

In [4]: series
Out[4]: 0     0
        1     1
        2     2
        3     3
        4     4
        5     5
```

The above prints a Pandas series with all values from the Numpy array – generated using the arange function – and the index. The output above shows the index of the Pandas series on the Left and the actual values on the right.

As we did not specify the index we want used, a default index made up of integers 0 through N − 1 - where N is the length of the data - is used. Using a Pandas series values and index attributes, we can also get the array representation and index object of the Pandas series.

```
In [8]: series.index
Out[8]: RangeIndex(start=0, stop=20, step=1)

In [7]: series.values # use value attribute
Out[7]: array([ 0,  1,  2,  3,  4,  5,  6,  7,  8,  9, 10, 11, 12, 13, 14, 15, 16,
               17, 18, 19])
```

The best way is to create a Pandas series with index identifying each data point with a specified data label as shown:

```
In [9]: indexed_Series = pd.Series([100,250,400,550,700], index=['OR','MI','MA','CA','VE'])

In [10]: indexed_Series
Out[10]: OR    100
         MI    250
         MA    400
         CA    550
         VE    700
         dtype: int64
```

For Pandas series, we can use the data labels in the index to select a single of a group of specific values.

```
In [12]: indexed_Series['CA']
Out[12]: 550
```

This case is also true while selecting multiple elements using their respective indices.

```
In [13]: indexed_Series[['CA','OR','MA']]
Out[13]: CA    550
         OR    100
         MA    400
         dtype: int64
```

In the code above, the arguments ['CA', 'OR,' 'MA] interpret as a list of indices although it contains string type instead of integers.

It is also good to note that using Numpy operations or Numpy-like operations such as logical filtering, scalar multiplication, or mathematical functions call will not alter the index values:

```
In [15]: np.exp(indexed_Series)
```

```
Out[15]: OR     2.688117e+43
         MI     3.746455e+108
         MA     5.221470e+173
         CA     7.277212e+238
         VE     1.014232e+304
         dtype: float64
```

As you can see, doing this preserves the indices of the elements while it subjects the actual values to a mathematical exponential function.

You can also think of a Pandas series as a dictionary of fixed length where the indices represent the keys of dictionaries and the actual values are the array elements. You can also pass a normal python dictionary to the Pandas Series function to create a series of elements.

```
In [19]: my_dict = {"OR": 100, "MI": 250, "MA": 400, "CA": 550, "VE": 700}
```

```
In [20]: pd.Series(my_dict)
```

```
Out[20]: OR     100
         MI     250
         MA     400
         CA     550
         VE     700
         dtype: int64
```

A Pandas series assigns a value of NaN (Not a Number) to missing values. If a value is missing an index, the Pandas Series does not include it. We use the functions isnull and notnull to detect missing data.

```
In [21]: indexed_Series.isnull()

Out[21]: OR     False
         MI     False
         MA     False
         CA     False
         VE     False
         dtype: bool
```

You can pass a new list of indices to alter the values assigned to the Pandas series as shown below:

```
In [22]: indexed_Series.index = ['A','B','C','D','E']

In [23]: indexed_Series

Out[23]: A    100
         B    250
         C    400
         D    550
         E    700
         dtype: int64
```

Python For Data Analysis

Pandas DataFrame

A Pandas DataFrame is probably the most used data structure offered by Pandas. A Pandas DataFrame is a rectangular table that contains an ordered collection of columns. A DataFrame column can each consist of different data types such as Booleans, strings, integers, etc. Unlike a series, a Pandas DataFrame has both rows and column indices. The best way to think of a Pandas as a DataFrame is like a spreadsheet document, or, on a more technical side, a dictionary of Pandas series sharing a unique index.

The most common way to create a Pandas DataFrame is by passing a python dictionary that contains equal length lists or a Numpy array to the DataFrame function.

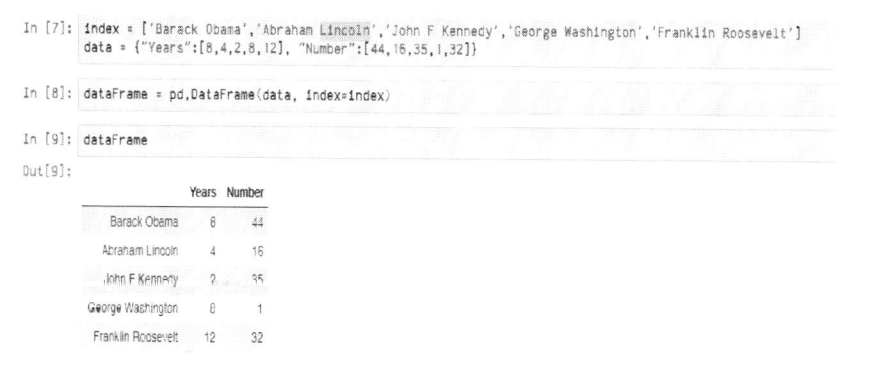

```
In [7]: index = ['Barack Obama','Abraham Lincoln','John F Kennedy','George Washington','Franklin Roosevelt']
        data = {"Years":[8,4,2,8,12], "Number":[44,16,35,1,32]}

In [8]: dataFrame = pd.DataFrame(data, index=index)

In [9]: dataFrame
Out[9]:
                      Years  Number
Barack Obama            8      44
Abraham Lincoln         4      16
John F Kennedy          2      35
George Washington       8       1
Franklin Roosevelt     12      32
```

First, we create a list containing the most popular presidents in the USA. Next, we create a dictionary containing their service years and the number which they served as president.

Finally, we pass the data to the DataFrame function and their names as the index for the data. That results in a data frame containing the names of the presidents as the index, their service years and column 1 and their service number as column 2.

NOTE: Use Jupyter notebook while working with DataFrames as the formatting is friendly —HTML.

If you have a large DataFrame, you can use the head function to grab the first 5 elements of the entire data. Like a Pandas Series, if you create a Pandas DataFrame with a missing DataFrame, it will fill up with NaN values:

```
In [15]: dataFrame = pd.DataFrame(data,columns=['Presidents','Years','Number'])

In [16]: dataFrame
Out[16]:
   Presidents  Years  Number
0         NaN      8      44
1         NaN      4      16
2         NaN      2      35
3         NaN      8       1
4         NaN     12      32
```

To retrieve a column in a Pandas DataFrame, we use either the dictionary notation —where we use the column name by using the attribute.

```
In [22]: dataFrame['Presidents']
Out[22]: 0          Barack Obama
         1       Abraham Lincoln
         2        John F Kennedy
         3     George Washington
         4    Franklin Roosevelt
         Name: Presidents, dtype: object
```

```
In [24]: dataFrame.Presidents
Out[24]: 0          Barack Obama
         1       Abraham Lincoln
         2        John F Kennedy
         3     George Washington
         4    Franklin Roosevelt
         Name: Presidents, dtype: object
```

Note that retrieving a column from a Pandas DataFrame produces a Pandas Series with its unique indices. This shows that a Pandas DataFrame consists of many Pandas Series. If you call the type function off the column, you will get a Pandas.core.series.Series data type.

```
In [25]: type(dataFrame.Presidents)
Out[25]: pandas.core.series.Series
```

We can also retrieve the rows of a Pandas DataFrame using a special loc attribute.

Python For Data Analysis

```
In [16]: dataFrame.loc['Abraham Lincoln']
Out[16]: Years     4
         Number   16
         Name: Abraham Lincoln, dtype: int64
```

NOTE: Depending on the method you use to execute the code used in the book, you might need to use the row number instead of the president's name and vice versa.

You can modify the Pandas dataframe columns by creating new ones and adding values to them. Let us add state column in our President's DataFrame as shown:

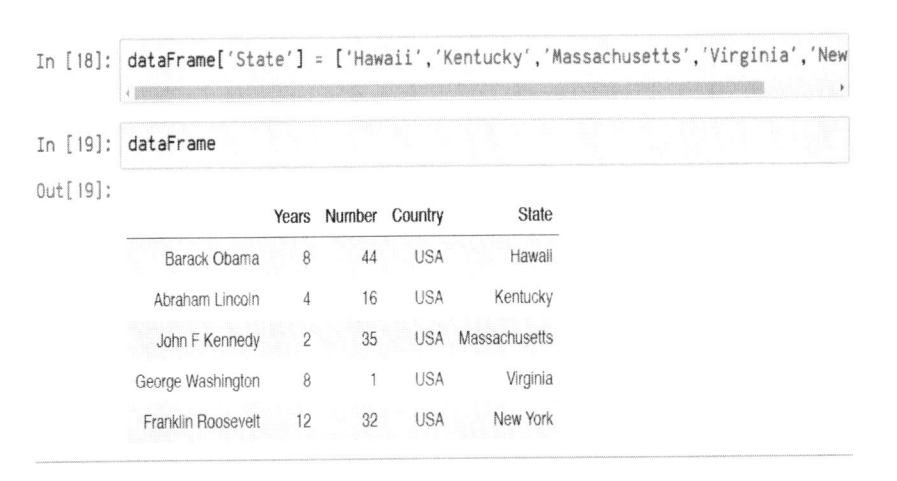

```
In [18]: dataFrame['State'] = ['Hawaii','Kentucky','Massachusetts','Virginia','New
```

```
In [19]: dataFrame
Out[19]:
```

	Years	Number	Country	State
Barack Obama	8	44	USA	Hawaii
Abraham Lincoln	4	16	USA	Kentucky
John F Kennedy	2	35	USA	Massachusetts
George Washington	8	1	USA	Virginia
Franklin Roosevelt	12	32	USA	New York

We pass the columns we want to add as a list followed by their corresponding values in respective order. Ensure to match the length of the DataFrame while assigning lists or arrays to a column to prevent occasions of missing data.

It is also important to note that assigning values to columns that do not exist will automatically create the column and assign to it the specified value.

To delete a column within a Pandas DataFrame, we use the del keyword, which is similar to how we delete a python dictionary. To illustrate column deletion, let us add a column called California and fill it with Boolean values – true if a president is from California and False if not.

```
In [21]: dataFrame['california'] = dataFrame.State == 'California'

In [22]: dataFrame
Out[22]:
```

	Years	Number	Country	State	california
Barack Obama	8	44	USA	Hawaii	False
Abraham Lincoln	4	16	USA	Kentucky	False
John F Kennedy	2	35	USA	Massachusetts	False
George Washington	8	1	USA	Virginia	False
Franklin Roosevelt	12	32	USA	New York	False

Using the del keyword, we can remove this column as shown below:

```
In [23]: del dataFrame['california']
```

```
In [24]: dataFrame
Out[24]:
```

	Years	Number	Country	State
Barack Obama	8	44	USA	Hawaii
Abraham Lincoln	4	16	USA	Kentucky
John F Kennedy	2	35	USA	Massachusetts
George Washington	8	1	USA	Virginia
Franklin Roosevelt	12	32	USA	New York

Now if we look at the existing columns within the DataFrame, we get four main columns as:

```
In [25]: dataFrame.columns
Out[25]: Index(['Years', 'Number', 'Country', 'State'], dtype='object')
```

Upon performing the del operation on the DataFrame, the returned column contains an actual view of the underlying data, which means that the operation occurs in-place, and any modifications undertaken on a section of the Pandas series also broadcasts to the original DataFrame.

You can copy a part of the Pandas array using the copy method. If a DataFrame does not have index and column name set, you can use the name attribute to accomplish this as shown below:

```
In [37]: dataFrame.index.name = ''; dataFrame.columns.name='Name'

In [38]: dataFrame
Out[38]:
```

Name	Years	Number	Country	State
Barack Obama	8	44	USA	Hawaii
Abraham Lincoln	4	16	USA	Kentucky
John F Kennedy	2	35	USA	Massachusetts
George Washington	8	1	USA	Virginia
Franklin Roosevelt	12	32	USA	New York

To get the values contained in a DataFrame, you can use the values attribute which returns a two-dimensional Numpy ndarrays, which is similar to the Pandas Series.

```
In [40]: dataFrame.values
Out[40]: array([[8, 44, 'USA', 'Hawaii'],
        [4, 16, 'USA', 'Kentucky'],
        [2, 35, 'USA', 'Massachusetts'],
        [8, 1, 'USA', 'Virginia'],
        [12, 32, 'USA', 'New York']], dtype=object)
```

In a scenario where the DataFrame's columns are of different data types, the data type of the values array is automatically set to accommodate all the columns in the DataFrame.

Now that we have discussed one of the most common ways to create a Pandas, let us look at some of the other types you can pass to the DataFrame function to create the DataFrame.

- A dictionary of dictionaries: Converts each inner dictionary to columns and merges the keys to form a row index.

- Two-dimensional Numpy array: Creates a DataFrame using the passed data. You can pass row and column labels but this optional.

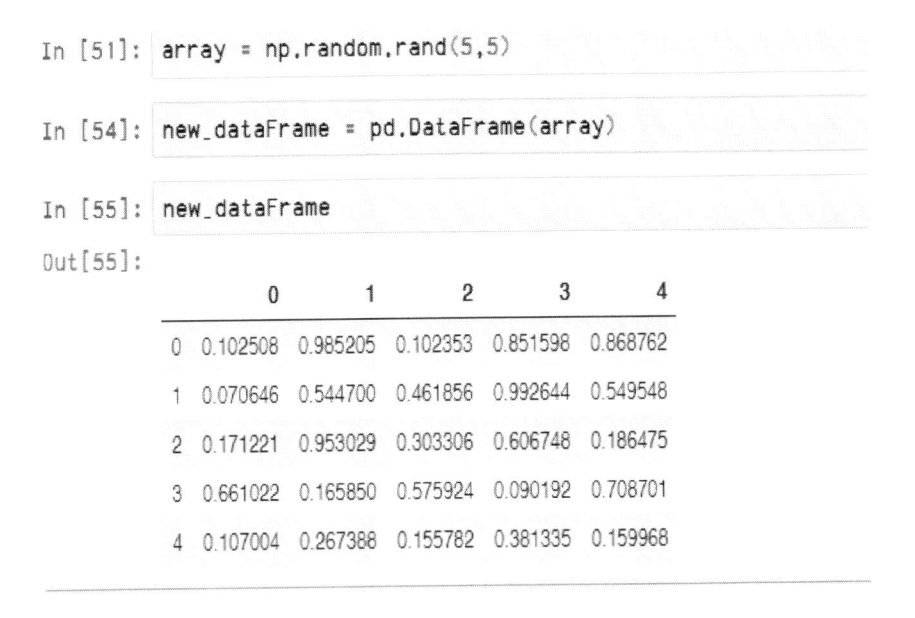

```
In [51]: array = np.random.rand(5,5)

In [54]: new_dataFrame = pd.DataFrame(array)

In [55]: new_dataFrame
Out[55]:
             0         1         2         3         4
   0  0.102508  0.985205  0.102353  0.851598  0.868762
   1  0.070646  0.544700  0.461856  0.992644  0.549548
   2  0.171221  0.953029  0.303306  0.606748  0.186475
   3  0.661022  0.165850  0.575924  0.090192  0.708701
   4  0.107004  0.267388  0.155782  0.381335  0.159968
```

- Numpy Masked Array

- Another Pandas DataFrame

- List of dictionaries

- List of series

- Numpy Structured array

Pandas Index objects

Pandas DataFrame indices are responsible for holding the axis labels and they included metadata of the entire DataFrame. Pandas automatically convert the sequence of labels or arrays passed to the DataFrame indices. For example, in the presidents' DataFrame, it automatically converts the names of the Presidents to become the DataFrame indices.

Since Pandas DataFrames are immutable, this makes it easy to share the DataFrames indices with other data structures. They, however, do not behave entirely like python sets in the sense that they can contain duplicate values. It is also good to note that the indices return in an array-like format while they are Pandas Index objects.

```
In [20]: dataFrame.index
Out[20]: Index(['Barack Obama', 'Abraham Lincoln', 'John F Kennedy',
               'George Washington', 'Franklin Roosevelt'],
              dtype='object', name='')

In [21]: type(dataFrame.index)
Out[21]: pandas.core.indexes.base.Index
```

Each index contains a set of methods and properties used to provide information about the data it contains. The most common ones include:

- Append: Concatenates multiple Indices objects, creating a new Index

- Difference: returns set difference as an Index

- Intersection: returns a set intersection

- Union: Returns set union

- Delete: Calculates a new Index with the element at index i deleted

- Drop: Returns a new Index by deleting passed values

- Insert: Returns a new Index by adding an element at index i

- is_monotonic: Returns true whenever a particular is greater than or equal to the previous element.

- is_unique: Returns Boolean True if the Index has no duplicate values.

- Unique: Returns the array of unique values in the Index

To delete on or more entries from Pandas DataFrame axes, we use the drop function, which returns a new DataFrame object with the specified values removed from the axes.

```
In [22]: dataFrame.drop('Franklin Roosevelt')
Out[22]:
```

	Name	Years	Number	State
	Barack Obama	8	44	Hawaii
	Abraham Lincoln	4	16	Kentucky
	John F Kennedy	2	35	Massachusetts
	George Washington	8	1	Virginia

It is imperative to note that calling the drop function deletes the values from the labels – i.e., axis = 0. If you want to delete values on a specific axis, you can pass it explicitly, which deletes the column.

In [46]: `copy_dataFrame.drop('Number', axis=1)`

Out[46]:

Name	Years	State
Barack Obama	8	Hawaii
Abraham Lincoln	4	Kentucky
John F Kennedy	2	Massachusetts
George Washington	8	Virginia
Franklin Roosevelt	12	New York

Since operations such as drop occur in-place to the original DataFrame, you should create a copy of the original DataFrame to avoid data loss. You can also specify in-place as False to prevent the changes from applying to the original DataFrame.

In [47]: `dataFrame.drop('Number', axis=1, inplace=False)`

Out[47]:

Name	Years	State
Barack Obama	8	Hawaii
Abraham Lincoln	4	Kentucky
John F Kennedy	2	Massachusetts
George Washington	8	Virginia
Franklin Roosevelt	12	New York

In [48]: `dataFrame`

Out[48]:

Name	Years	Number	State
Barack Obama	8	44	Hawaii
Abraham Lincoln	4	16	Kentucky
John F Kennedy	2	35	Massachusetts
George Washington	8	1	Virginia
Franklin Roosevelt	12	32	New York

Indexing, Selection, and Slicing

We can use the Pandas series indexing technique to select subsections of the Pandas DataFrame. Example:

```
In [57]: dataFrame["Years"]
Out[57]:
        Barack Obama            8
        Abraham Lincoln         4
        John F Kennedy          2
        George Washington       8
        Franklin Roosevelt      12
        Name: Years, dtype: int64
```

NOTE: This only selects the integral section of the DataFrame.

Slicing a Pandas data structure, however, behaves differently from the usual python slicing technique as the end value is inclusive.

Missing Data In Pandas

Cases of missing data are especially common while working with external data. Although we usually clean and recheck data from sources such as Kaggle, data from sources such as logs and spreadsheets may have some missing data.

If Pandas encounter missing data, it automatically assigns the value Not a Number value (NaN). In real-world cases, missing data is very problematic and can cause inaccurate results. Fortunately, Pandas provide functions that allow us to check for missing data within a specified DataFrame. These functions are isnull() and notnull().

These two functions return a Boolean value where the two cases are true or false. In cases where you have missing data, you can manually fill in the data or use Pandas built-in functions to generate random but similar data.

Functions such as replace(), fillna() or interpolate() and dropna() provide the ability to delete or fill the missing data within the data frame, which saves lots of time compared to manually entering the data and dealing with the errors that may occur due to missing data.

We use the dropna() function to remove the rows and columns that have missing data in the DataFrame. The table below shows the most common Pandas DataFrame methods.

DataFrame Function	Function Operation
isnull()	Checks for missing values in a DataFrame and returns Boolean true for true cases

notnull()	Checks for missing values and returns false where there is no missing data
where()	Checks DataFrame for a given condition
rename()	Used to rename indexes of columns and rows in a DataFrame
fillna()	Allows users to specify the filling value for missing data
copy()	Creates a copy of Pandas objects
drop_duplicates	Filters and removes duplicates in a Pandas DataFrame
set_index()	Used to set index of DataFrame rows
reset_index()	Resets the indexes in a Pandas DataFrame
insert()	Inserts new columns in a DataFrame
values()	Returns a DataFrame without axes and labels —it's more like a Numpy array

Working With External Data Sources

In the real world, you will rarely work with randomly generated data. Instead, you will be using external data sources from spreadsheets and program logs. Accessing external data is an essential data science skill.

In this section, we are going to look at the most common ways to read and output data in external sources. We will be using Pandas; however, other python libraries can perform this task better. The table below shows the main Pandas functions used to read external data.

Function name	Function Operation
read_csv()	Used to read delimited data from a file, web URL and file-like object using a comma delimiter
read_html()	Used to read table attributes in a html file
read_pickle()	Used to read arbitrary objects stored in pickle formats https://docs.python.org/3/library/pickle.html

`read_table()`	Used to read delimited data from file, URL, and file-like objects using \t (tab) delimiter
`read_excel()`	Used to fetch tabulated data from excel formats such as XLS and XLSX
`read_json()`	Used to read data from JavaScript Object Notation format (JSON)
`read_msgpack()`	Used to read Pandas data encoded in MessagePack binary format. https://msgpack.org/index.html
`read_sql()`	Used to read data from a SQL database query and return it as a Pandas DataFrame. It requires the installation of the SQLAlchemy library. https://pypi.org/project/SQLAlchemy/
`read-stata()`	Used to read data stored in stata file format. https://Pandas.pydata.org/Pandas-docs/stable/reference/api/Pandas.r

	ead_stata.html
read_sas()	Reads a SAS dataset stored in the SAS system's custom storage formats
read_feather()	Used to read feather binary data format
read_hdf()	Read HDF5 files written by Pandas
read_clipboard()	Used to read supported data that is stored in the system clipboard
read_fwf()	Used to read data in fixed-width column format – data that do not contain delimiters

Most of these functions such as read_csv have developed over time and can support more than 50 parameters, which usually occurs due to misconfiguration of world data and very messy data sources.

To learn more about these functions. Navigate to the Pandas official documentation available here:

https://Pandas.pydata.org/Pandas-docs/stable/

Chapter 7: Data Wrangling

As mentioned, in the real world, you will have to interact with various data sources and very messy data. Since you will fetch the data from different applications and databases, its arrangement and configuration will be different on each application. For example, data from Postgresql will be different from data from Microsoft Excel. Data from various sources is complicated to clean and analyze.

In this section, we are going to deal with data wrangling, a process that involves combining, joining, and rearranging data from different sources so that we can analyze it easily.

First, we will discuss a critical concept in Pandas and data wrangling: *hierarchical indexing.*

Hierarchical Indexing

Hierarchical Indexing in Pandas is a feature that allows you to work with higher dimensional data in lower dimensional form. This Pandas feature enables you to have multi-dimensional (two or more) index levels on a data axis.

We will start by creating a simple Pandas Series with indexes.

```
In [5]: my_data = pd.Series(np.random.randn(10),index=[['w','w','w','x','x','x','y','y','z','z'],[10,20,30,10,10,30,10,10,30,10,20,20,:

In [6]: my_data
Out[6]: w  10   -0.208380
           20    0.277941
           30    0.251286
        x  10   -0.150518
           10    0.234399
           30    1.479576
        y  10    0.061534
           20    0.009757
        z  20    0.725877
           30    0.633856
        dtype: float64
```

The above code shows an example of hierarchical indexing. The distance between the indices the separates the indices. For example, index W contains 10 values, which are indices, and each index in w (and others) has its respective value. Hierarchical indexing allows you to select subsets of data concisely.

```
In [10]: my_data[['w','x']]
Out[10]: w  10   -0.208380
            20    0.277941
            30    0.251286
         x  10   -0.150518
            10    0.234399
            30    1.479576
         dtype: float64
```

You can also choose data from the inner sections of the Series. For example, we can use the .loc attribute.

```
In [16]: my_data.loc[:, [10,20]]
Out[16]: w  10   -0.208380
            20    0.277941
         x  10   -0.150518
            10    0.234399
         y  10    0.061534
            20    0.009757
         z  20    0.725877
         dtype: float64
```

We use this indexing technique extensively in reshaping data and group-based operations such as the formation of a pivot table. We can accomplish this using a stack and unstack method. Depending on the data used to call the method, these methods will produce errors if they contain duplicate values.

With Pandas DataFrame, each of its axes can have a hierarchical index. While working with hierarchical indexing, you may want to reset or change the current indices of the data. You can accomplish this by using the reset_index and set_index respectively.

Dataset Merge & Combining Operations

There are two main ways of combining data stored in a Pandas data structure. They include (Remember pd represent Pandas):

Python For Data Analysis

- pd.concat – used to stack or concatenate Pandas objects along the axis

```
In [15]: df1 = pd.DataFrame({'A': ['A0', 'A1', 'A2', 'A3'],
                             'B': ['B0', 'B1', 'B2', 'B3'],
                             'C': ['C0', 'C1', 'C2', 'C3'],
                             'D': ['D0', 'D1', 'D2', 'D3']},
                            index = [0, 1, 2, 3])
```

```
In [16]: df2 = pd.DataFrame({'A': ['A4', 'A5', 'A6', 'A7'],
                             'B': ['B4', 'B5', 'B6', 'B7'],
                             'C': ['C4', 'C5', 'C6', 'C7'],
                             'D': ['D4', 'D5', 'D6', 'D7']},
                            index = [4, 5, 6, 7])
```

```
In [17]: df3 = pd.DataFrame({'A': ['A8', 'A9', 'A10', 'A11'],
                             'B': ['B8', 'B9', 'B10', 'B11'],
                             'C': ['C8', 'C9', 'C10', 'C11'],
                             'D': ['D8', 'D9', 'D10', 'D11']},
                            index = [8, 9, 10, 11])
```

Using the Pandas concact method, we can combine all the data frames above to create one data frame as shown below:

```
In [20]: pd.concat([df3,df2,df1])
Out[20]:
```

	A	B	C	D
8	A8	B8	C8	D8
9	A9	B9	C9	D9
10	A10	B10	C10	D10
11	A11	B11	C11	D11
4	A4	B4	C4	D4
5	A5	B5	C5	D5
6	A6	B6	C6	D6
7	A7	B7	C7	D7
0	A0	B0	C0	D0
1	A1	B1	C1	D1
2	A2	B2	C2	D2
3	A3	B3	C3	D3

- pd.merge – We use the Pandas merge function to combine data by connecting the rows in the DataFrame based on one or more keys. If you are familiar with SQL or any relational database, this method is similar to a join operation.

```
In [27]: pd.merge(df2,df1)
Out[27]:
            A  B  C  D
```

In the above example, we did not specify which columns of the DataFrame to merge. If this occurs, the merge functions overlap the column names and used them as keys. We can see this in the above example. It is, therefore, a good practice to specify which columns should merge with which (ended with adjective - fix).

If the column names are not similar on both data frames, you can specify them explicitly using the right_on and left_on arguments. This is an example of many-to-one merge.

You may notice that the produced DataFrame contains only the merged columns while it associated data is missing. This occurs due to merge functions performing an inner merge operation. Hence the keys are intersected and only the common values are found on both.

In [34]: `df5 = pd.merge(df2,df1,how='right')`

In [35]: `df5`

Out[35]:

	A	B	C	D
0	A0	B0	C0	D0
1	A1	B1	C1	D1
2	A2	B2	C2	D2
3	A3	B3	C3	D3

You can use the how argument to specify how the merge operations is done. The accepted arguments are: inner, right, left, outer and output.

Permutations and Random Sampling

Mathematically, permutations refer to the process of rearranging sets into a sequence or reordering its elements. We can perform permutation operations on Pandas Series or DataFrames using the np.random.permuation function. This function takes the length of the axis as an argument and returns an array of integer values in a new ordered sequence.

Chapter 8: Data Visualization With Matplotlib

Data visualization is the graphical analysis and interpretation of scientific data with the aim of making better decisions. In python, data visualization involves using scientific libraries and packages to represent data visually for better interpretation.

The following are the most important elements you need to have in mind to work with Python data visualization

Matplotlib

Matplotlib is a python plotting library that allows you to create visual representations of data such as graphs, heat maps, and more in 2D. As we discussed in earlier sections, Matplotlib has the same MATLAB graphical capabilities and provides complete control of the figures plotted. Matplotlib works efficiently with Pandas DataFrames and Numpy Arrays. By convention, we import Matplotlib as plt using the code below:

```
import matplotlib.pyplot as plt

%Matplotlib inline
```

Python For Data Analysis

We use the code %Matplotlib inline to make the statistical plots display upon code execution in the jupyter notebook, which will only work if you are using the Jupyter notebook as your code editor. However, if you are not working with jupyter notebook, enter the command plt.show() at the end of every plot.

Let us begin by importing Numpy and Pandas. Next, create two arrays using either of the methods we learned in the previous chapters. In the example below, we create an array x with 11 linearly spaced points from 5 to 10. The array y contains the x values exponent to power of 3.

```
In [2]: import pandas as pd
        import numpy as np

In [3]: x = np.linspace(5, 10, 10)
        y = x ** 3

In [5]: x
Out[5]: array([ 5.        ,  5.55555556,  6.11111111,  6.66666667,  7.22222222,
                7.77777778,  8.33333333,  8.88888889,  9.44444444, 10.        ])

In [6]: y
Out[6]: array([ 125.        ,  171.46776406,  228.22359396,  296.2962963 ,
                376.71467764,  470.50754458,  578.7037037 ,  702.33196159,
                842.42112483, 1000.        ])
```

To create Matplotlib plots, we can use the functional method or the Object-Oriented method. It is important to have OOP knowledge to tackle this method.

The functional method involves various plotting functions and passing the points as the arguments. For example, we can create basic plot as:

```
In [8]: plt.plot(y,x)
Out[8]: [<matplotlib.lines.Line2D at 0x1cd9293bd88>]
```

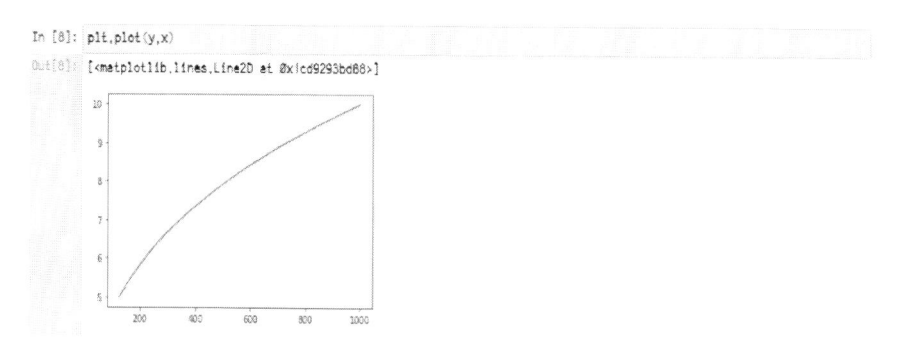

If you are familiar with Matlab, you can pass similar arguments to the plots such as color and line style.

If we want to add labels to the Matplotlib plots, we can use the functions such as xlabel, ylabel and title as shown below.

```
plt.plot(y,x)
plt.xlabel('X')
plt.ylabel('Y')
plt.title('Plot of Y vs X')
Text(0.5, 1.0, 'Plot of Y vs X')
```

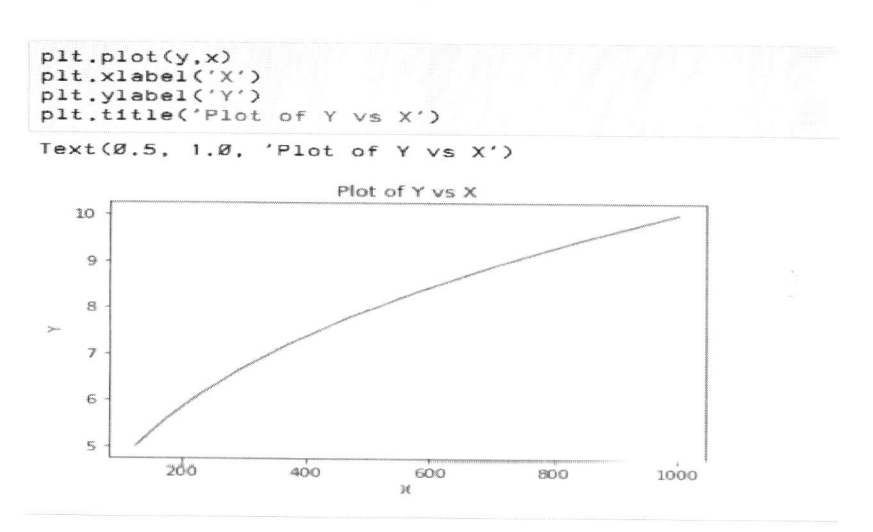

If we want to create multiple plots on the same canvas, we can do this using the subplot function. This function takes in various arguments such as number of rows, number of columns and the plot number respectively.

For example:

```
plt.subplot(1,2,1)
plt.plot(x,y,'g')

plt.subplot(1,2,2)
plt.plot(y,x,'r')
```

[<matplotlib.lines.Line2D at 0x1cd9394ca08>]

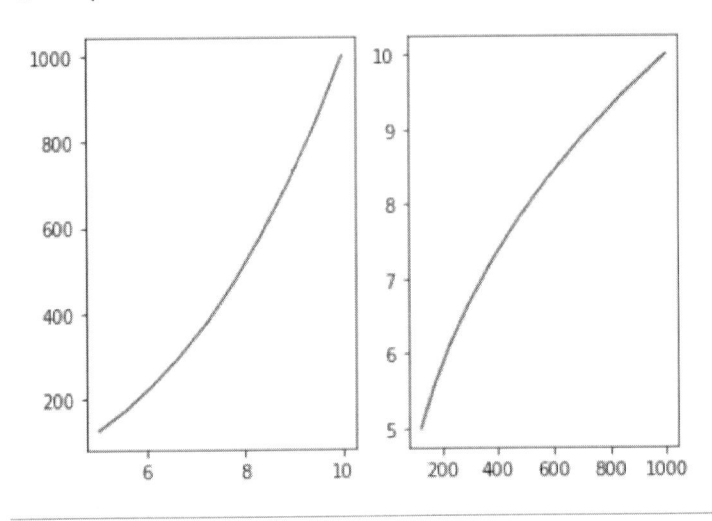

Matplotlib allows you to have different representation of the same data. Similar to MATLAB (for those familiar), Matplotlib allows you to plot various types of plots on the given data. These types of plots include:

- Bar plots

- Histograms

- Scatter Plots

To plot a bar plot using Matplotlib, we pass the data we want plotted inside the plt.bar() function as shown below.

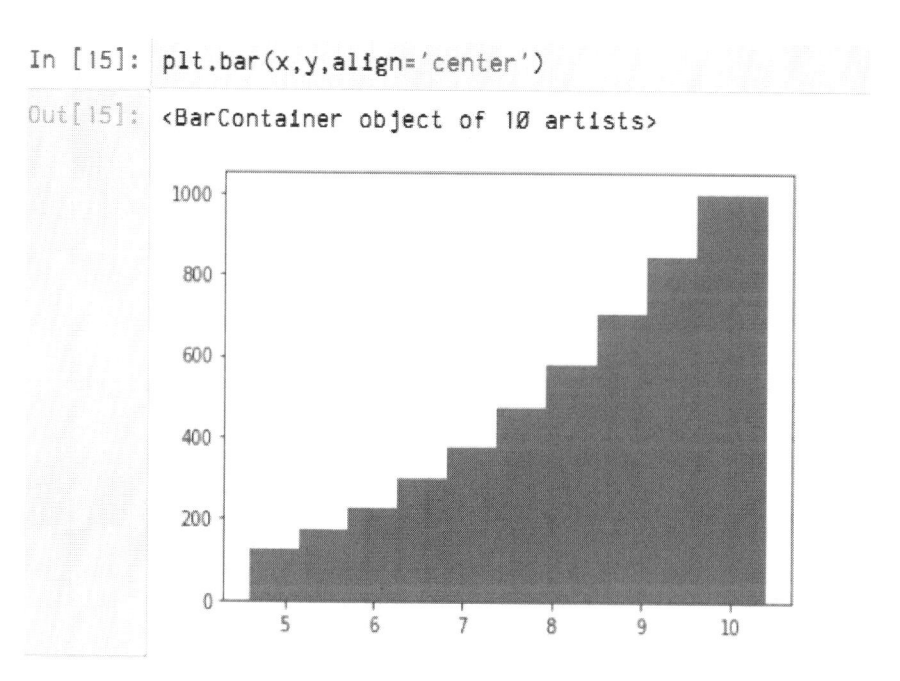

```
In [15]: plt.bar(x,y,align='center')
Out[15]: <BarContainer object of 10 artists>
```

You can pass other arguments inside the function to modify how the plot appears. In the Jupyter notebook, you can find more information about a specific function by pressing SHIFT + TAB. This gives a brief documentation about the method.

```
plt.bar()

Signature:
plt.bar(
    x,
    height,
    width=0.8,
    bottom=None,
    *,
    align='center',
    data=None,
    **kwargs,
```

Plotting a histogram using Matplotlib is similar to the bar plot where we use the plt.hist() function.

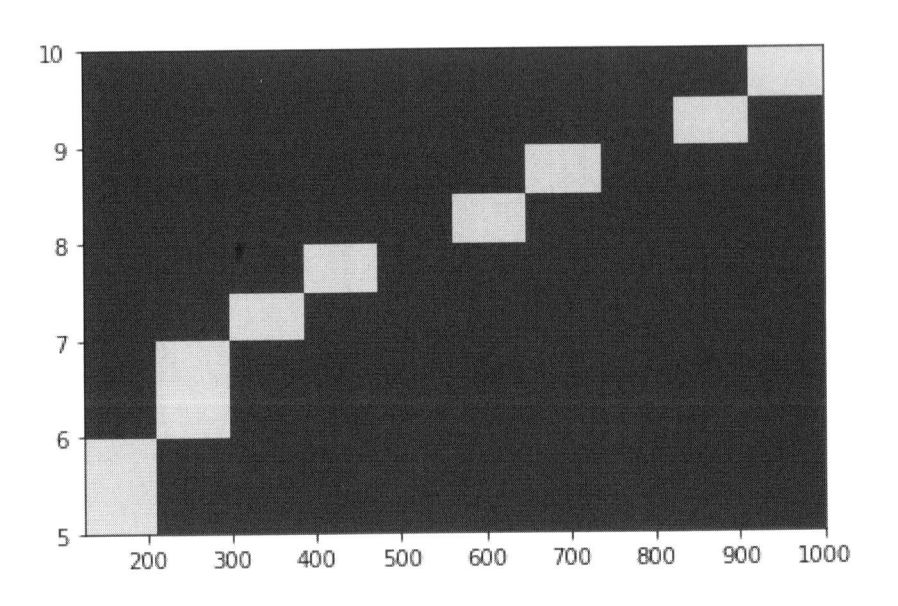

To plot scatter plots, we use the plt.scatter() function passing the data we want plotted inside the function.

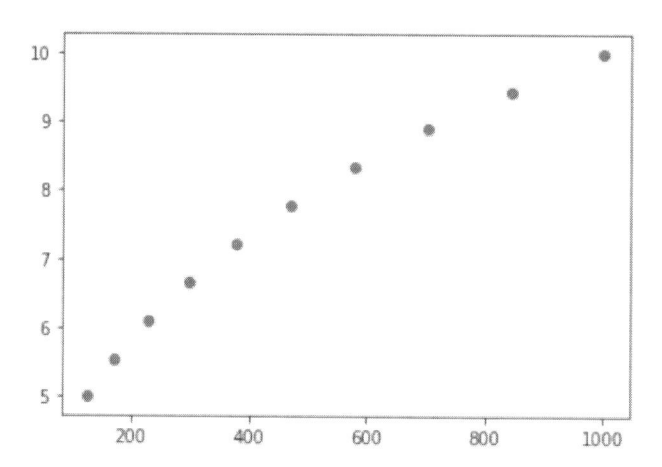

```
plt.scatter(y,x)
```
<matplotlib.collections.PathCollection at 0x111e2f6a3c8>

Matplotlib is a complex and essential library that is inexhaustable within the scope of this book. You can find more information about Matplotlib and its plotting capabilities on the official documentation available here

https://Matplotlib.org/contents.html

Pandas Built-In Visualization

Here, we are going to go over the Pandas built-in data visualization capabilities.

Although Pandas is a data analysis library, it offers some data visualization features mainly built over Matplotlib. It is good to note that Matplotlib and Pandas do not offer very advanced plotting and visualization features compared to libraries such as Seaborn —not covered in the book.

Let us start by creating two Pandas DataFrames using any of the methods discussed in previous chapters. For this example, we will import Pandas sample csv files. You can get sample data from.

https://www.kaggle.com/

```
In [2]: dataFrame1 = pd.read_csv('df1',index_col=0)
```

```
In [5]: dataFrame2 = pd.read_csv('df2')
```

After the creation of the DataFrames, we can start creating various plots. For example, to create a histogram of the values in column 'A' of dataFrame1, we use: dataFrame1['A'].hist()

```
In [7]: dataFrame1['A'].hist()
Out[7]: <matplotlib.axes._subplots.AxesSubplot at 0x1e222ab7788>
```

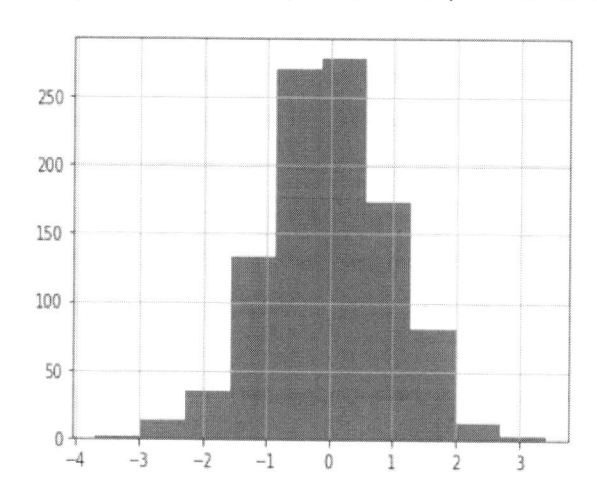

If you look carefully, you will notice that Pandas is referencing Matplotlib for this plots. This means that you can pass Matplotlib plots arguments such as color and bins.

This method calls the type of plot off the DataFrame column. You can use the entire DataFrame (not recommended due to performance issues).

```
dataFrame2.hist()
array([[<matplotlib.axes._subplots.AxesSubplot object at 0x0000001E224107348>,
        <matplotlib.axes._subplots.AxesSubplot object at 0x0000001E22410EDC8>],
       [<matplotlib.axes._subplots.AxesSubplot object at 0x0000001E22516FB88>,
        <matplotlib.axes._subplots.AxesSubplot object at 0x0000001E2251A95C8>]],
      dtype=object)
```

Other kind of plots you can perform off panda DataFrames directly include:

- Area plot: This takes in various arguments such as x and y although not mandatory. The general syntax is:

`DataFrame.plot.area(self, x=, y=, **kwargs)`

- Bar plots

- Line plots

- Scatter plots

- Box plots

- Kernel density estimation plots

```
dataFrame2.plot.kde()
```

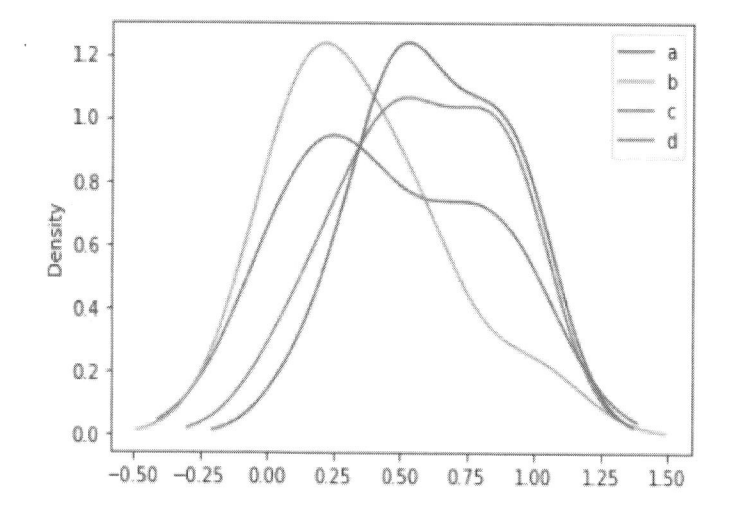

<matplotlib.axes._subplots.AxesSubplot at 0x1e2254f0908>

Conclusion

We have completed our tutorial on data analysis using python.

As mentioned earlier, if you do not have python programming knowledge or statistical computations, you will struggle with understanding some aspects of the book.

The following are the recommend skills you should have before getting into data science:

- Python Programming

- Databases: Relational databases at most (MySQL, Oracle etc)

- Statistical Computation: Recommend reading, Introduction to Statistical Learning with Applications in R by Gareth James.

Thank you for reading this guide. I hope you found it immensely valuable.

I'd like your feedback. If you are happy with this book, please leave a review on Amazon.

Please leave a review for this book on Amazon by visiting the page below:

Python For Data Analysis

https://amzn.to/2VMR5qr

Printed in Great Britain
by Amazon